MW01443452

WORD

A Guided Journal for
Listening to God

DONNA SUTHERLAND NORMAN

WORD: A Guided Journal for Listening to God

Copyright © 2023. Donna L. Norman

All rights Reserved. No part of this book may be reproduced or transmitted in any form or by any means, electronic or mechanical, including photocopying, recording, or by any information storage and retrieval system, without permission in writing from the publisher or author.

ISBN: 978-1-7371856-0-4

Printed in the United States of America

DEDICATION

I dedicate this journal to my husband, Pelsby, and to my children Jacob, Leah, and Caleb. I thank God for placing you in my life as the fuel to my fire.

This journal provides direction for the time after your "AMEN." After you submit your prayer, it is important to listen for God's response. Through intentional focus, you start to see what God is revealing to you.

The WORD Journal is a space for commune and strengthening your intimacy with Him. He will share His ideas, visions, feelings, corrections, and directions with you. He may speak to you through feelings or heart tugs, experiences, people, scriptures, words, books, etc. The most important part of this journaling experience is paying attention. When you pay attention, you see, hear and learn.

Communing with God or communion is a two-sided conversation. If you are always talking or praying and never pausing to listen, you miss the revelation. When you are in conversation, you talk then listen. You listen then respond.

Journaling gives room for all that God wants to reveal to you. Through recording His revelations in this journal you notice more and more confirmations of His word. You will position yourself to live out His word more confidently differentiating His voice from your own voice.

"Call to Me, and I will answer you, and show you great and mighty things, which you do not know."

- Jeremiah 33:3 NKJV

WHY DID I CREATE THIS JOURNAL?

I often struggle with hearing from God. As I grew in my faith and started to hear from God, I started putting some practices in place to ensure that I was taking advantage of this special relationship. Most of this came through lessons from failed experiences or trial and error. Like when God gave me a word to share and I forgot about it. Life happened, I got busy, and I forgot. Not being able to act immediately, didn't mean don't act at all. I realized that I needed a place to store the things that He was placing on my heart and in my head.

I am the type of person who talks to God wherever and whenever. We are always in conversation whether I am driving in my car, resting in bed, or in a time of dedicated prayer. I use the word conversation loosely because most of the time, I was doing the talking and telling God what I wanted, needed, or wished. My other realization was that He would provide more direction if I gave him space to talk to me. I shifted from just talking to God to concentrated time listening to Him. Simply, stating "speak to me Lord" or "help me understand" then I would just listen.

In her book "Fervent Prayer", Priscilla Shirer provides a prayer structure that works well for me. Praise - Repent - Ask - Yield. I was really good about praising and asking, not so bad about repenting but yielding. What did it look like to yield? This journal provides a space to yield.

WHAT DOES IT MEAN TO LISTEN?

There are two types of listening to be discussed here, passive and active listening.

Passive listening is when we hear what God is speaking but we don't react or respond to what he is saying. Amy reads her Bible everyday and she knows God's word. Amy does not see any changes in her life because she is not consciously applying God's word to her life. Amy would be a passive listener.

Now let's talk about Cynthia. Like Amy, Cynthia reads her Bible everyday and she knows God's word. Unlike Amy, Cynthia is purposeful about applying God's word by listening for what the Word is speaking to her. Cynthia is an active listener. Active listening is when we hear what God is saying, we are fully engaged and responding to His word.

Passive listening is one-way communication while active listening is two-way communication. This journal is designed to help you to enhance your relationship with God through active listening.

The way to improve your listening skills is to practice "active listening." This is applicable with people and with God. In order to do this you need to be purposeful and fully attentive. Remove distractions, avoid limiting beliefs, and stay focused. Here are some key principles of active listening:

Pay Attention - "Remember this, my dear brothers and sisters: Everyone should be quick to listen, slow to speak, and should not get angry easily." - James 1:19 GW

Withhold Judgement - "For the Father judgeth no man, but hath committed all judgement unto the Son." - John 5:22 KJV

Reflect - Meditate upon these things; give thyself wholly to them; that thy profiting may appear to all." - 1 Timothy 4:15 KJV

Clarify - "For God is not the author of confusion, but of peace, as in all churches of the saints." - 1 Corinthians 14:33 KJV

Let It Sink In - "For the word of God is quick, and powerful, and sharper than any two-edged sword, piercing even to the dividing asunder of soul and spirit, and of the joints and marrow, and is a discerner of the thoughts and intents of the heart." - Hebrews 4:12 KJV

HOW TO USE THIS JOURNAL?

Choose Your Word - Choose your word based on an issue or thought that has been weighing on your heart. Keep it to a single word that speaks to an area where you desire to hear from God. This is not about hearing God's word from the Bible, but hearing God's specific instruction for you as it relates to the concern in your heart.

> **EXAMPLE**
>
> You are struggling with work and you are unsure of the direction or path to take. You may feel the need to speak with your supervisor about your position or career path. Think about what you are seeking. You may want to say that you are seeking career growth or perhaps clarity in direction. So your word might be growth, clarity or direction. For this purpose, we will use the word, clarity.

Asking of God - In this area you will write to God, specifically what you are seeking during your listening time.

> **EXAMPLE**
>
> God, I am asking you for clarity on the best approach in discussing my career with my supervisor. Please help me to understand what to say, when to say it. Help me to communicate in a way that he is able to receive what I am saying with grace and understanding.

Meditative Support - In this area you will identify a scripture or quote, a song to support your listening time with God.

What does meditative mean? The adjective meditative is good for describing something that's reflective or deeply thoughtful. The root of meditative is the Latin word meditat, or "contemplated," which in turn comes from a Proto-Indo-European root that means "to measure, consider, or advise." When you reflect on your life or an important decision, you are meditative, and anything that involves this state of mind can be described the same way.

https://www.vocabulary.com/dictionary/meditative

EXAMPLE
Scripture on clarity: "And your ears shall hear a word behind you, saying, 'This is the way, walk in it,' when you turn to the right or when you turn to the left." - Isaiah 30:21
Meditative song: "Just Haven't Seen It" by Danny Gokey

Journaling What You Hear - God speaks in a variety of ways. This is an experience that is unique to you because your relationship with God is unique. Honor that about your relationship. Many people seek an audible voice when hearing from God, while this may happen, it is not the only way that God might speak to you. Listen with your heart and your head.

Use this space to write what you hear, what you feel, what you say...anything or way that you feel God is connecting you to your word. I choose not to be prescriptive because I believe God will lead and guide your time with him. Just as he orders your steps, he will order your writing.

Write what comes to your mind without restriction. Write without restriction. Write without judgement. Write what you feel, hear or see that is connecting you to your word. Pay attention and remember to practice active listening. It may help to seek out a quiet space to gather your thoughts, reflect on your experiences, and thoughts. If you at all are uncertain, ask God to give you clarity. As you reflect on your writings, look for connections and seek meaning.

Revelation Report - This space is an area for you to celebrate your revelations based on your journaling experience.

This listening journal is designed to be a week-long experience. This takes the pressure off of rushing the experience and it provides time for you to go deep with your journaling and reflections.

"Remember this, my dear brothers and sisters: Everyone should be quick to listen, slow to speak, and should not get angry easily."

- James 1:19 GW

DATE _____

My word this week is _____

God, I am asking you _____

_____

_____

_____

_____

_____

Daily Prayer: Father God. I come before you and I humble myself in your presence. Thank you for being ever present in my life. Forgive me for anything in my heart that is not like you. I ask you to hear the word of my heart. As I meditate on this word, please reveal your Word to me through scripture, song and Your voice. Speak to me as only you can. In Jesus' name I pray. Amen

Meditative Scripture/Quote: _____

_____

_____

_____

_____

Meditative Song: _____

What do you hear God saying to you?

_____

_____

_____

_____

_____

_____

_____

_____

_____

_____

_____

_____

_____

_____

Revelation report _____

_____

_____

DATE _____

My word this week is _____

God, I am asking you _____

_____

_____

_____

_____

Daily Prayer: Father God. I come before you and I humble myself in your presence. Thank you for being ever present in my life. Forgive me for anything in my heart that is not like you. I ask you to hear the word of my heart. As I meditate on this word, please reveal your Word to me through scripture, song and Your voice. Speak to me as only you can. In Jesus' name I pray. Amen

Meditative Scripture/Quote: _____

_____

_____

_____

Meditative Song: _____

What do you hear God saying to you?

_____

_____

_____

_____

_____

_____

_____

_____

_____

_____

_____

_____

_____

_____

_____

Revelation report _____

_____

_____

DATE _____

My word this week is _____

God, I am asking you _____

_____

_____

_____

_____

_____

Daily Prayer: Father God. I come before you and I humble myself in your presence. Thank you for being ever present in my life. Forgive me for anything in my heart that is not like you. I ask you to hear the word of my heart. As I meditate on this word, please reveal your Word to me through scripture, song and Your voice. Speak to me as only you can. In Jesus' name I pray. Amen

Meditative Scripture/Quote: _____

_____

_____

_____

_____

Meditative Song: _____

What do you hear God saying to you?

_____

_____

_____

_____

_____

_____

_____

_____

_____

_____

_____

_____

_____

_____

Revelation report _____

_____

_____

DATE _____

My word this week is _____

God, I am asking you _____

_____

_____

_____

_____

Daily Prayer: Father God. I come before you and I humble myself in your presence. Thank you for being ever present in my life. Forgive me for anything in my heart that is not like you. I ask you to hear the word of my heart. As I meditate on this word, please reveal your Word to me through scripture, song and Your voice. Speak to me as only you can. In Jesus' name I pray. Amen

Meditative Scripture/Quote: _____

_____

_____

_____

Meditative Song: _____

What do you hear God saying to you?

_____

_____

_____

_____

_____

_____

_____

_____

_____

_____

_____

_____

_____

_____

_____

_____

Revelation report _____

_____

_____

DATE _____

My word this week is _____

God, I am asking you _____

_____

_____

_____

_____

_____

Daily Prayer: Father God. I come before you and I humble myself in your presence. Thank you for being ever present in my life. Forgive me for anything in my heart that is not like you. I ask you to hear the word of my heart. As I meditate on this word, please reveal your Word to me through scripture, song and Your voice. Speak to me as only you can. In Jesus' name I pray. Amen

Meditative Scripture/Quote: _____

_____

_____

_____

_____

Meditative Song: _____

What do you hear God saying to you?

_____

_____

_____

_____

_____

_____

_____

_____

_____

_____

_____

_____

_____

_____

Revelation report _____

_____

_____

DATE _____

My word this week is _____

God, I am asking you _____

_____

_____

_____

_____

_____

Daily Prayer: Father God. I come before you and I humble myself in your presence. Thank you for being ever present in my life. Forgive me for anything in my heart that is not like you. I ask you to hear the word of my heart. As I meditate on this word, please reveal your Word to me through scripture, song and Your voice. Speak to me as only you can. In Jesus' name I pray. Amen

Meditative Scripture/Quote: _____

_____

_____

_____

_____

Meditative Song: _____

What do you hear God saying to you?

_____

_____

_____

_____

_____

_____

_____

_____

_____

_____

_____

_____

_____

Revelation report _____

_____

_____

DATE _____

My word this week is _____

God, I am asking you _____

_____

_____

_____

_____

_____

Daily Prayer: Father God. I come before you and I humble myself in your presence. Thank you for being ever present in my life. Forgive me for anything in my heart that is not like you. I ask you to hear the word of my heart. As I meditate on this word, please reveal your Word to me through scripture, song and Your voice. Speak to me as only you can. In Jesus' name I pray. Amen

Meditative Scripture/Quote: _____

_____

_____

_____

_____

Meditative Song: _____

What do you hear God saying to you?

_____
_____
_____
_____
_____
_____
_____
_____
_____
_____
_____
_____
_____
_____
_____
_____
_____
_____

Revelation report _____
_____
_____

DATE _____

My word this week is _____

God, I am asking you _____

_____

_____

_____

_____

_____

Daily Prayer: Father God. I come before you and I humble myself in your presence. Thank you for being ever present in my life. Forgive me for anything in my heart that is not like you. I ask you to hear the word of my heart. As I meditate on this word, please reveal your Word to me through scripture, song and Your voice. Speak to me as only you can. In Jesus' name I pray. Amen

Meditative Scripture/Quote: _____

_____

_____

_____

Meditative Song: _____

What do you hear God saying to you?

_____
_____
_____
_____
_____
_____
_____
_____
_____
_____
_____
_____
_____
_____

Revelation report _____
_____
_____

DATE _____

My word this week is _____

God, I am asking you _____

_____

_____

_____

_____

_____

Daily Prayer: Father God. I come before you and I humble myself in your presence. Thank you for being ever present in my life. Forgive me for anything in my heart that is not like you. I ask you to hear the word of my heart. As I meditate on this word, please reveal your Word to me through scripture, song and Your voice. Speak to me as only you can. In Jesus' name I pray. Amen

Meditative Scripture/Quote: _____

_____

_____

_____

_____

Meditative Song: _____

What do you hear God saying to you?

_____

_____

_____

_____

_____

_____

_____

_____

_____

_____

_____

_____

_____

_____

Revelation report _____

_____

_____

DATE _____

My word this week is _____

God, I am asking you _____

_____

_____

_____

_____

_____

Daily Prayer: Father God. I come before you and I humble myself in your presence. Thank you for being ever present in my life. Forgive me for anything in my heart that is not like you. I ask you to hear the word of my heart. As I meditate on this word, please reveal your Word to me through scripture, song and Your voice. Speak to me as only you can. In Jesus' name I pray. Amen

Meditative Scripture/Quote: _____

_____

_____

_____

_____

Meditative Song: _____

What do you hear God saying to you?

_____

_____

_____

_____

_____

_____

_____

_____

_____

_____

_____

_____

_____

_____

_____

Revelation report _____

_____

_____

DATE _____

My word this week is _____

God, I am asking you _____

_____

_____

_____

_____

Daily Prayer: Father God. I come before you and I humble myself in your presence. Thank you for being ever present in my life. Forgive me for anything in my heart that is not like you. I ask you to hear the word of my heart. As I meditate on this word, please reveal your Word to me through scripture, song and Your voice. Speak to me as only you can. In Jesus' name I pray. Amen

Meditative Scripture/Quote: _____

_____

_____

_____

Meditative Song: _____

What do you hear God saying to you?

_____

_____

_____

_____

_____

_____

_____

_____

_____

_____

_____

_____

_____

Revelation report _____

_____

_____

DATE _____

My word this week is _____

God, I am asking you _____

_____

_____

_____

_____

_____

Daily Prayer: Father God. I come before you and I humble myself in your presence. Thank you for being ever present in my life. Forgive me for anything in my heart that is not like you. I ask you to hear the word of my heart. As I meditate on this word, please reveal your Word to me through scripture, song and Your voice. Speak to me as only you can. In Jesus' name I pray. Amen

Meditative Scripture/Quote: _____

_____

_____

_____

_____

Meditative Song: _____

What do you hear God saying to you?

_____
_____
_____
_____
_____
_____
_____
_____
_____
_____
_____
_____
_____
_____
_____
_____
_____
_____

Revelation report _____
_____
_____

DATE _____

My word this week is _____

God, I am asking you _____

_____

_____

_____

_____

Daily Prayer: Father God. I come before you and I humble myself in your presence. Thank you for being ever present in my life. Forgive me for anything in my heart that is not like you. I ask you to hear the word of my heart. As I meditate on this word, please reveal your Word to me through scripture, song and Your voice. Speak to me as only you can. In Jesus' name I pray. Amen

Meditative Scripture/Quote: _____

_____

_____

_____

_____

Meditative Song: _____

What do you hear God saying to you?

_____
_____
_____
_____
_____
_____
_____
_____
_____
_____
_____
_____
_____
_____
_____

Revelation report _____

_____
_____

DATE _____

YOU DID IT!
Quarterly Check-In

Quarterly Prayer: Thank you Lord for giving yourself through the gift of the Holy Spirit. I am grateful to you for opening my eyes, mind, and heart as I learn to enjoy your presence. Lord, please continue to speak to me in ways that I can understand. Show me how I might share your presence with others. Amen

Set aside some quiet time to review the last quarter of your journaling using the following writing prompts.

What were some key moments of revelation?_____

_____

_____

_____

_____

_____

_____

What have you learned about yourself and your relationship with God?_____

_____

_____

_____

_____

_____

How will you celebrate this accomplishment? _____

_____

_____

_____

_____

_____

_____

"Therefore, my beloved brothers, be steadfast, immovable, always abounding in the work of the Lord, knowing that in the Lord your labor is not in vain."

- 1 Corinthians 15:58 NKJV

DATE _____

My word this week is _____

God, I am asking you _____

_____

_____

_____

_____

_____

Daily Prayer: Father God. I come before you and I humble myself in your presence. Thank you for being ever present in my life. Forgive me for anything in my heart that is not like you. I ask you to hear the word of my heart. As I meditate on this word, please reveal your Word to me through scripture, song and Your voice. Speak to me as only you can. In Jesus' name I pray. Amen

Meditative Scripture/Quote: _____

_____

_____

_____

_____

Meditative Song: _____

What do you hear God saying to you?

_____
_____
_____
_____
_____
_____
_____
_____
_____
_____
_____
_____
_____
_____

Revelation report _____
_____
_____

DATE _____

My word this week is _____

God, I am asking you _____

_____

_____

_____

_____

_____

Daily Prayer: Father God. I come before you and I humble myself in your presence. Thank you for being ever present in my life. Forgive me for anything in my heart that is not like you. I ask you to hear the word of my heart. As I meditate on this word, please reveal your Word to me through scripture, song and Your voice. Speak to me as only you can. In Jesus' name I pray. Amen

Meditative Scripture/Quote: _____

_____

_____

_____

_____

Meditative Song: _____

What do you hear God saying to you?

_____
_____
_____
_____
_____
_____
_____
_____
_____
_____
_____
_____
_____
_____
_____

Revelation report _____
_____
_____

DATE _____

My word this week is _____

God, I am asking you _____

_____

_____

_____

_____

Daily Prayer: Father God. I come before you and I humble myself in your presence. Thank you for being ever present in my life. Forgive me for anything in my heart that is not like you. I ask you to hear the word of my heart. As I meditate on this word, please reveal your Word to me through scripture, song and Your voice. Speak to me as only you can. In Jesus' name I pray. Amen

Meditative Scripture/Quote: _____

_____

_____

_____

_____

Meditative Song: _____

What do you hear God saying to you?

_____

_____

_____

_____

_____

_____

_____

_____

_____

_____

_____

_____

_____

_____

Revelation report _____

_____

_____

DATE _____

My word this week is _____

God, I am asking you _____

_____

_____

_____

_____

_____

Daily Prayer: Father God. I come before you and I humble myself in your presence. Thank you for being ever present in my life. Forgive me for anything in my heart that is not like you. I ask you to hear the word of my heart. As I meditate on this word, please reveal your Word to me through scripture, song and Your voice. Speak to me as only you can. In Jesus' name I pray. Amen

Meditative Scripture/Quote: _____

_____

_____

_____

_____

Meditative Song: _____

What do you hear God saying to you?

_____
_____
_____
_____
_____
_____
_____
_____
_____
_____
_____
_____
_____
_____
_____

Revelation report _____
_____
_____

DATE _____

My word this week is _____

God, I am asking you _____

_____

_____

_____

_____

_____

Daily Prayer: Father God. I come before you and I humble myself in your presence. Thank you for being ever present in my life. Forgive me for anything in my heart that is not like you. I ask you to hear the word of my heart. As I meditate on this word, please reveal your Word to me through scripture, song and Your voice. Speak to me as only you can. In Jesus' name I pray. Amen

Meditative Scripture/Quote: _____

_____

_____

_____

_____

Meditative Song: _____

What do you hear God saying to you?

_____
_____
_____
_____
_____
_____
_____
_____
_____
_____
_____
_____
_____
_____
_____

Revelation report _____
_____
_____

DATE _____

My word this week is _____

God, I am asking you _____

_____

_____

_____

_____

Daily Prayer: Father God. I come before you and I humble myself in your presence. Thank you for being ever present in my life. Forgive me for anything in my heart that is not like you. I ask you to hear the word of my heart. As I meditate on this word, please reveal your Word to me through scripture, song and Your voice. Speak to me as only you can. In Jesus' name I pray. Amen

Meditative Scripture/Quote: _____

_____

_____

_____

_____

Meditative Song: _____

What do you hear God saying to you?

_____

_____

_____

_____

_____

_____

_____

_____

_____

_____

_____

_____

_____

_____

_____

Revelation report _____

_____

_____

DATE _____

My word this week is _____

God, I am asking you _____

_____

_____

_____

_____

Daily Prayer: Father God. I come before you and I humble myself in your presence. Thank you for being ever present in my life. Forgive me for anything in my heart that is not like you. I ask you to hear the word of my heart. As I meditate on this word, please reveal your Word to me through scripture, song and Your voice. Speak to me as only you can. In Jesus' name I pray. Amen

Meditative Scripture/Quote: _____

_____

_____

_____

_____

Meditative Song: _____

What do you hear God saying to you?

_____
_____
_____
_____
_____
_____
_____
_____
_____
_____
_____
_____
_____
_____
_____
_____
_____

Revelation report _____
_____
_____

DATE _____

My word this week is _____

God, I am asking you _____

_____

_____

_____

_____

Daily Prayer: Father God. I come before you and I humble myself in your presence. Thank you for being ever present in my life. Forgive me for anything in my heart that is not like you. I ask you to hear the word of my heart. As I meditate on this word, please reveal your Word to me through scripture, song and Your voice. Speak to me as only you can. In Jesus' name I pray. Amen

Meditative Scripture/Quote: _____

_____

_____

_____

_____

Meditative Song: _____

What do you hear God saying to you?

_____

_____

_____

_____

_____

_____

_____

_____

_____

_____

_____

_____

_____

_____

_____

_____

_____

Revelation report _____

_____

_____

DATE _____

My word this week is _____

God, I am asking you _____

_____

_____

_____

_____

_____

Daily Prayer: Father God. I come before you and I humble myself in your presence. Thank you for being ever present in my life. Forgive me for anything in my heart that is not like you. I ask you to hear the word of my heart. As I meditate on this word, please reveal your Word to me through scripture, song and Your voice. Speak to me as only you can. In Jesus' name I pray. Amen

Meditative Scripture/Quote: _____

_____

_____

_____

_____

Meditative Song: _____

What do you hear God saying to you?

_____
_____
_____
_____
_____
_____
_____
_____
_____
_____
_____
_____
_____
_____

Revelation report _____
_____
_____

DATE _____

My word this week is _____

God, I am asking you _____

_____

_____

_____

_____

_____

Daily Prayer: Father God. I come before you and I humble myself in your presence. Thank you for being ever present in my life. Forgive me for anything in my heart that is not like you. I ask you to hear the word of my heart. As I meditate on this word, please reveal your Word to me through scripture, song and Your voice. Speak to me as only you can. In Jesus' name I pray. Amen

Meditative Scripture/Quote: _____

_____

_____

_____

_____

Meditative Song: _____

What do you hear God saying to you?

_____

_____

_____

_____

_____

_____

_____

_____

_____

_____

_____

_____

_____

Revelation report _____

_____

_____

DATE _____

My word this week is _____

God, I am asking you _____

_____

_____

_____

_____

_____

Daily Prayer: Father God. I come before you and I humble myself in your presence. Thank you for being ever present in my life. Forgive me for anything in my heart that is not like you. I ask you to hear the word of my heart. As I meditate on this word, please reveal your Word to me through scripture, song and Your voice. Speak to me as only you can. In Jesus' name I pray. Amen

Meditative Scripture/Quote: _____

_____

_____

_____

_____

Meditative Song: _____

What do you hear God saying to you?

_____
_____
_____
_____
_____
_____
_____
_____
_____
_____
_____
_____
_____
_____
_____
_____

Revelation report _____
_____
_____

DATE _____

My word this week is _____

God, I am asking you _____

_____

_____

_____

_____

_____

Daily Prayer: Father God. I come before you and I humble myself in your presence. Thank you for being ever present in my life. Forgive me for anything in my heart that is not like you. I ask you to hear the word of my heart. As I meditate on this word, please reveal your Word to me through scripture, song and Your voice. Speak to me as only you can. In Jesus' name I pray. Amen

Meditative Scripture/Quote: _____

_____

_____

_____

_____

Meditative Song: _____

What do you hear God saying to you?

_____

_____

_____

_____

_____

_____

_____

_____

_____

_____

_____

_____

_____

_____

_____

Revelation report _____

_____

_____

DATE _____

My word this week is _____

God, I am asking you _____

_____

_____

_____

_____

_____

Daily Prayer: Father God. I come before you and I humble myself in your presence. Thank you for being ever present in my life. Forgive me for anything in my heart that is not like you. I ask you to hear the word of my heart. As I meditate on this word, please reveal your Word to me through scripture, song and Your voice. Speak to me as only you can. In Jesus' name I pray. Amen

Meditative Scripture/Quote: _____

_____

_____

_____

_____

Meditative Song: _____

What do you hear God saying to you?

_____
_____
_____
_____
_____
_____
_____
_____
_____
_____
_____
_____
_____
_____

Revelation report _____
_____
_____

DATE _____

WINNING MINDSET!
Quarterly Check-In

Quarterly Prayer: Thank you Lord for giving yourself through the gift of the Holy Spirit. I am grateful to you for opening my eyes, mind, and heart as I learn to enjoy your presence. Lord, please continue to speak to me in ways that I can understand. Show me how I might share your presence with others. Amen

Set aside some quiet time to review the last quarter of your journaling using the following writing prompts.

What were some key moments of revelation?_____

_____

_____

_____

_____

_____

_____

What have you learned about yourself and your relationship with God?_____

_____

_____

_____

_____

_____

How will you celebrate this accomplishment? _____

_____

_____

_____

_____

_____

"And let us not grow weary while doing good, for in due season we shall reap, if we don't lose heart."

- Galations 6:9 NKJV

DATE _____

My word this week is _____

God, I am asking you _____

_____

_____

_____

_____

Daily Prayer: Father God. I come before you and I humble myself in your presence. Thank you for being ever present in my life. Forgive me for anything in my heart that is not like you. I ask you to hear the word of my heart. As I meditate on this word, please reveal your Word to me through scripture, song and Your voice. Speak to me as only you can. In Jesus' name I pray. Amen

Meditative Scripture/Quote: _____

_____

_____

_____

_____

Meditative Song: _____

What do you hear God saying to you?

_____

_____

_____

_____

_____

_____

_____

_____

_____

_____

_____

_____

_____

Revelation report _____

_____

_____

DATE _____

My word this week is _____

God, I am asking you _____

_____

_____

_____

_____

_____

Daily Prayer: Father God. I come before you and I humble myself in your presence. Thank you for being ever present in my life. Forgive me for anything in my heart that is not like you. I ask you to hear the word of my heart. As I meditate on this word, please reveal your Word to me through scripture, song and Your voice. Speak to me as only you can. In Jesus' name I pray. Amen

Meditative Scripture/Quote: _____

_____

_____

_____

_____

Meditative Song: _____

What do you hear God saying to you?

_____
_____
_____
_____
_____
_____
_____
_____
_____
_____
_____
_____
_____

Revelation report _____
_____
_____

DATE _____

My word this week is _____

God, I am asking you _____

_____

_____

_____

_____

_____

Daily Prayer: Father God. I come before you and I humble myself in your presence. Thank you for being ever present in my life. Forgive me for anything in my heart that is not like you. I ask you to hear the word of my heart. As I meditate on this word, please reveal your Word to me through scripture, song and Your voice. Speak to me as only you can. In Jesus' name I pray. Amen

Meditative Scripture/Quote: _____

_____

_____

_____

_____

Meditative Song: _____

What do you hear God saying to you?

_____

_____

_____

_____

_____

_____

_____

_____

_____

_____

_____

_____

_____

Revelation report _____

_____

_____

DATE _____

My word this week is _____

God, I am asking you _____

_____

_____

_____

_____

_____

Daily Prayer: Father God. I come before you and I humble myself in your presence. Thank you for being ever present in my life. Forgive me for anything in my heart that is not like you. I ask you to hear the word of my heart. As I meditate on this word, please reveal your Word to me through scripture, song and Your voice. Speak to me as only you can. In Jesus' name I pray. Amen

Meditative Scripture/Quote: _____

_____

_____

_____

_____

Meditative Song: _____

What do you hear God saying to you?

_____

_____

_____

_____

_____

_____

_____

_____

_____

_____

_____

_____

_____

_____

_____

Revelation report _____

_____

_____

DATE _____

My word this week is _____

God, I am asking you _____

_____

_____

_____

_____

_____

Daily Prayer: Father God. I come before you and I humble myself in your presence. Thank you for being ever present in my life. Forgive me for anything in my heart that is not like you. I ask you to hear the word of my heart. As I meditate on this word, please reveal your Word to me through scripture, song and Your voice. Speak to me as only you can. In Jesus' name I pray. Amen

Meditative Scripture/Quote: _____

_____

_____

_____

_____

Meditative Song: _____

What do you hear God saying to you?

_____
_____
_____
_____
_____
_____
_____
_____
_____
_____
_____
_____
_____
_____

Revelation report _____
_____
_____

DATE _____

My word this week is _____

God, I am asking you _____

_____

_____

_____

_____

_____

Daily Prayer: Father God. I come before you and I humble myself in your presence. Thank you for being ever present in my life. Forgive me for anything in my heart that is not like you. I ask you to hear the word of my heart. As I meditate on this word, please reveal your Word to me through scripture, song and Your voice. Speak to me as only you can. In Jesus' name I pray. Amen

Meditative Scripture/Quote: _____

_____

_____

_____

_____

Meditative Song: _____

What do you hear God saying to you?

_____
_____
_____
_____
_____
_____
_____
_____
_____
_____
_____
_____
_____

Revelation report _____
_____
_____

DATE _____

My word this week is _____

God, I am asking you _____

_____

_____

_____

_____

_____

Daily Prayer: Father God. I come before you and I humble myself in your presence. Thank you for being ever present in my life. Forgive me for anything in my heart that is not like you. I ask you to hear the word of my heart. As I meditate on this word, please reveal your Word to me through scripture, song and Your voice. Speak to me as only you can. In Jesus' name I pray. Amen

Meditative Scripture/Quote: _____

_____

_____

_____

_____

Meditative Song: _____

What do you hear God saying to you?

___

___

___

___

___

___

___

___

___

___

___

___

___

___

___

___

Revelation report ___

___

___

DATE _____

My word this week is _____

God, I am asking you _____

_____

_____

_____

_____

_____

Daily Prayer: Father God. I come before you and I humble myself in your presence. Thank you for being ever present in my life. Forgive me for anything in my heart that is not like you. I ask you to hear the word of my heart. As I meditate on this word, please reveal your Word to me through scripture, song and Your voice. Speak to me as only you can. In Jesus' name I pray. Amen

Meditative Scripture/Quote: _____

_____

_____

_____

_____

Meditative Song: _____

What do you hear God saying to you?

___

Revelation report ___

DATE _____

My word this week is _____

God, I am asking you _____

_____

_____

_____

_____

_____

Daily Prayer: Father God. I come before you and I humble myself in your presence. Thank you for being ever present in my life. Forgive me for anything in my heart that is not like you. I ask you to hear the word of my heart. As I meditate on this word, please reveal your Word to me through scripture, song and Your voice. Speak to me as only you can. In Jesus' name I pray. Amen

Meditative Scripture/Quote: _____

_____

_____

_____

_____

Meditative Song: _____

What do you hear God saying to you?

_____

_____

_____

_____

_____

_____

_____

_____

_____

_____

_____

_____

_____

_____

_____

Revelation report _____

_____

_____

DATE _____

My word this week is _____

God, I am asking you _____

_____

_____

_____

_____

Daily Prayer: Father God. I come before you and I humble myself in your presence. Thank you for being ever present in my life. Forgive me for anything in my heart that is not like you. I ask you to hear the word of my heart. As I meditate on this word, please reveal your Word to me through scripture, song and Your voice. Speak to me as only you can. In Jesus' name I pray. Amen

Meditative Scripture/Quote: _____

_____

_____

_____

_____

Meditative Song: _____

What do you hear God saying to you?

_____

_____

_____

_____

_____

_____

_____

_____

_____

_____

_____

_____

_____

_____

Revelation report _____

_____

_____

DATE _____

My word this week is _____

God, I am asking you _____

_____

_____

_____

_____

_____

Daily Prayer: Father God. I come before you and I humble myself in your presence. Thank you for being ever present in my life. Forgive me for anything in my heart that is not like you. I ask you to hear the word of my heart. As I meditate on this word, please reveal your Word to me through scripture, song and Your voice. Speak to me as only you can. In Jesus' name I pray. Amen

Meditative Scripture/Quote: _____

_____

_____

_____

_____

Meditative Song: _____

What do you hear God saying to you?

_____

_____

_____

_____

_____

_____

_____

_____

_____

_____

_____

_____

_____

_____

Revelation report _____

_____

_____

DATE _____

My word this week is _____

God, I am asking you _____

_____

_____

_____

_____

_____

Daily Prayer: Father God. I come before you and I humble myself in your presence. Thank you for being ever present in my life. Forgive me for anything in my heart that is not like you. I ask you to hear the word of my heart. As I meditate on this word, please reveal your Word to me through scripture, song and Your voice. Speak to me as only you can. In Jesus' name I pray. Amen

Meditative Scripture/Quote: _____

_____

_____

_____

_____

Meditative Song: _____

What do you hear God saying to you?

Revelation report

DATE _____

My word this week is _____

God, I am asking you _____

_____

_____

_____

_____

_____

Daily Prayer: Father God. I come before you and I humble myself in your presence. Thank you for being ever present in my life. Forgive me for anything in my heart that is not like you. I ask you to hear the word of my heart. As I meditate on this word, please reveal your Word to me through scripture, song and Your voice. Speak to me as only you can. In Jesus' name I pray. Amen

Meditative Scripture/Quote: _____

_____

_____

_____

_____

Meditative Song: _____

What do you hear God saying to you?

_____
_____
_____
_____
_____
_____
_____
_____
_____
_____
_____
_____
_____
_____
_____

Revelation report _____
_____
_____

DATE _____

ROCK ON!
Quarterly Check-In

Quarterly Prayer: Thank you Lord for giving yourself through the gift of the Holy Spirit. I am grateful to you for opening my eyes, mind, and heart as I learn to enjoy your presence. Lord, please continue to speak to me in ways that I can understand. Show me how I might share your presence with others. Amen

Set aside some quiet time to review the last quarter of your journaling using the following writing prompts.

What were some key moments of revelation?_____

_____

_____

_____

_____

_____

_____

What have you learned about yourself and your relationship with God?_____

_____

_____

_____

_____

_____

How will you celebrate this accomplishment? _____

_____

_____

_____

_____

_____

_____

"Jesus Christ is the same yesterday, today, and forever."

- Hebrews 13:8 NKJV

DATE _____

My word this week is _____

God, I am asking you _____

_____

_____

_____

_____

_____

Daily Prayer: Father God. I come before you and I humble myself in your presence. Thank you for being ever present in my life. Forgive me for anything in my heart that is not like you. I ask you to hear the word of my heart. As I meditate on this word, please reveal your Word to me through scripture, song and Your voice. Speak to me as only you can. In Jesus' name I pray. Amen

Meditative Scripture/Quote: _____

_____

_____

_____

_____

Meditative Song: _____

What do you hear God saying to you?

_____
_____
_____
_____
_____
_____
_____
_____
_____
_____
_____
_____
_____
_____

Revelation report _____
_____
_____

DATE _____

My word this week is _____

God, I am asking you _____

_____

_____

_____

_____

_____

Daily Prayer: Father God. I come before you and I humble myself in your presence. Thank you for being ever present in my life. Forgive me for anything in my heart that is not like you. I ask you to hear the word of my heart. As I meditate on this word, please reveal your Word to me through scripture, song and Your voice. Speak to me as only you can. In Jesus' name I pray. Amen

Meditative Scripture/Quote: _____

_____

_____

_____

_____

Meditative Song: _____

What do you hear God saying to you?

_____

_____

_____

_____

_____

_____

_____

_____

_____

_____

_____

_____

_____

_____

_____

_____

Revelation report _____

_____

_____

DATE _____

My word this week is _____

God, I am asking you _____

_____

_____

_____

_____

_____

Daily Prayer: Father God. I come before you and I humble myself in your presence. Thank you for being ever present in my life. Forgive me for anything in my heart that is not like you. I ask you to hear the word of my heart. As I meditate on this word, please reveal your Word to me through scripture, song and Your voice. Speak to me as only you can. In Jesus' name I pray. Amen

Meditative Scripture/Quote: _____

_____

_____

_____

_____

Meditative Song: _____

What do you hear God saying to you?

_____
_____
_____
_____
_____
_____
_____
_____
_____
_____
_____
_____
_____
_____
_____

Revelation report _____
_____
_____

DATE _____

My word this week is _____

God, I am asking you _____

_____

_____

_____

_____

_____

Daily Prayer: Father God. I come before you and I humble myself in your presence. Thank you for being ever present in my life. Forgive me for anything in my heart that is not like you. I ask you to hear the word of my heart. As I meditate on this word, please reveal your Word to me through scripture, song and Your voice. Speak to me as only you can. In Jesus' name I pray. Amen

Meditative Scripture/Quote: _____

_____

_____

_____

_____

Meditative Song: _____

What do you hear God saying to you?

Revelation report _____

DATE _____

My word this week is _____

God, I am asking you _____

_____

_____

_____

_____

_____

Daily Prayer: Father God. I come before you and I humble myself in your presence. Thank you for being ever present in my life. Forgive me for anything in my heart that is not like you. I ask you to hear the word of my heart. As I meditate on this word, please reveal your Word to me through scripture, song and Your voice. Speak to me as only you can. In Jesus' name I pray. Amen

Meditative Scripture/Quote: _____

_____

_____

_____

_____

Meditative Song: _____

What do you hear God saying to you?

_____

_____

_____

_____

_____

_____

_____

_____

_____

_____

_____

_____

_____

_____

_____

Revelation report _____

_____

_____

DATE _____

My word this week is _____

God, I am asking you _____

_____

_____

_____

_____

Daily Prayer: Father God. I come before you and I humble myself in your presence. Thank you for being ever present in my life. Forgive me for anything in my heart that is not like you. I ask you to hear the word of my heart. As I meditate on this word, please reveal your Word to me through scripture, song and Your voice. Speak to me as only you can. In Jesus' name I pray. Amen

Meditative Scripture/Quote: _____

_____

_____

_____

_____

Meditative Song: _____

What do you hear God saying to you?

_____

_____

_____

_____

_____

_____

_____

_____

_____

_____

_____

_____

_____

_____

_____

_____

Revelation report _____

_____

_____

DATE _____

My word this week is _____

God, I am asking you _____

_____

_____

_____

_____

Daily Prayer: Father God. I come before you and I humble myself in your presence. Thank you for being ever present in my life. Forgive me for anything in my heart that is not like you. I ask you to hear the word of my heart. As I meditate on this word, please reveal your Word to me through scripture, song and Your voice. Speak to me as only you can. In Jesus' name I pray. Amen

Meditative Scripture/Quote: _____

_____

_____

_____

_____

Meditative Song: _____

What do you hear God saying to you?

Revelation report _____

DATE _____

My word this week is _____

God, I am asking you _____

_____

_____

_____

_____

_____

Daily Prayer: Father God. I come before you and I humble myself in your presence. Thank you for being ever present in my life. Forgive me for anything in my heart that is not like you. I ask you to hear the word of my heart. As I meditate on this word, please reveal your Word to me through scripture, song and Your voice. Speak to me as only you can. In Jesus' name I pray. Amen

Meditative Scripture/Quote: _____

_____

_____

_____

_____

Meditative Song: _____

What do you hear God saying to you?

_____

_____

_____

_____

_____

_____

_____

_____

_____

_____

_____

_____

_____

Revelation report _____

_____

_____

DATE _____

My word this week is _____

God, I am asking you _____

_____

_____

_____

_____

_____

Daily Prayer: Father God. I come before you and I humble myself in your presence. Thank you for being ever present in my life. Forgive me for anything in my heart that is not like you. I ask you to hear the word of my heart. As I meditate on this word, please reveal your Word to me through scripture, song and Your voice. Speak to me as only you can. In Jesus' name I pray. Amen

Meditative Scripture/Quote: _____

_____

_____

_____

_____

Meditative Song: _____

What do you hear God saying to you?

_____
_____
_____
_____
_____
_____
_____
_____
_____
_____
_____
_____
_____
_____

Revelation report _____
_____
_____

DATE _____

My word this week is _____

God, I am asking you _____

_____

_____

_____

_____

Daily Prayer: Father God. I come before you and I humble myself in your presence. Thank you for being ever present in my life. Forgive me for anything in my heart that is not like you. I ask you to hear the word of my heart. As I meditate on this word, please reveal your Word to me through scripture, song and Your voice. Speak to me as only you can. In Jesus' name I pray. Amen

Meditative Scripture/Quote: _____

_____

_____

_____

_____

Meditative Song: _____

What do you hear God saying to you?

_____

_____

_____

_____

_____

_____

_____

_____

_____

_____

_____

Revelation report _____

_____

_____

DATE _____

My word this week is _____

God, I am asking you _____

_____

_____

_____

_____

_____

Daily Prayer: Father God. I come before you and I humble myself in your presence. Thank you for being ever present in my life. Forgive me for anything in my heart that is not like you. I ask you to hear the word of my heart. As I meditate on this word, please reveal your Word to me through scripture, song and Your voice. Speak to me as only you can. In Jesus' name I pray. Amen

Meditative Scripture/Quote: _____

_____

_____

_____

_____

Meditative Song: _____

What do you hear God saying to you?

_____

_____

_____

_____

_____

_____

_____

_____

_____

_____

_____

_____

Revelation report _____

_____

_____

DATE _____

My word this week is _____

God, I am asking you _____

_____

_____

_____

_____

_____

Daily Prayer: Father God. I come before you and I humble myself in your presence. Thank you for being ever present in my life. Forgive me for anything in my heart that is not like you. I ask you to hear the word of my heart. As I meditate on this word, please reveal your Word to me through scripture, song and Your voice. Speak to me as only you can. In Jesus' name I pray. Amen

Meditative Scripture/Quote: _____

_____

_____

_____

_____

Meditative Song: _____

What do you hear God saying to you?

_____

_____

_____

_____

_____

_____

_____

_____

_____

_____

_____

_____

_____

_____

Revelation report _____

_____

_____

DATE _____

My word this week is _____

God, I am asking you _____

_____

_____

_____

_____

_____

Daily Prayer: Father God. I come before you and I humble myself in your presence. Thank you for being ever present in my life. Forgive me for anything in my heart that is not like you. I ask you to hear the word of my heart. As I meditate on this word, please reveal your Word to me through scripture, song and Your voice. Speak to me as only you can. In Jesus' name I pray. Amen

Meditative Scripture/Quote: _____

_____

_____

_____

_____

Meditative Song: _____

What do you hear God saying to you?

_____
_____
_____
_____
_____
_____
_____
_____
_____
_____
_____
_____
_____
_____

Revelation report _____
_____
_____

CONGRATULATIONS!!

You committed to and completed 52-weeks of tuning into God's voice. You did not grow weary. You remained consistent in your focus on listening to what God is communicating to you.

"And let us not grow weary of doing good, for in due season we will reap, if we do not give up." Galatians 6:9 ESV

Studies show that when you do something for 30 days, it will become a habit and if you do it for 90 days it becomes a way of life. You have surpassed that by completing 52 weekly sessions just between you and God. By now, I pray that you are well-tuned into His voice and how it shows up in your life. I pray that He has revealed to you all that you have been seeking to glean from Him.

The practice not only helps you in your prayer life but more importantly increases clarity on how God shows up in your life. Personally, it has brought me more joy and improved alignment with my purpose. It is amazing the revelation when you take time to listen. It is alarming to think about how much you miss when you spend more time talking to God in prayer than you spend listening for his response to your prayer. **I recommend you read Samuel's story in 1 Samuel 3:10.** Continue to challenge yourself in making God's voice louder than your voice.

'If anyone has ears to hear, let him hear. And he said to them, "Pay attention to what you hear: with the measure you use it, it will be measured to you, and still more will be added to you.' Mark 4:23-24 ESV

What are your final reflections about this journey of practicing active listening in your relationship with God?

_____

_____

_____

_____

_____

_____

_____

How will you celebrate this accomplishment? _____

_____

_____

_____

_____

_____

_____

"Jesus Christ is the same yesterday, today, and forever."

- *Hebrews 13:8 NKJV*

Concept By: Donna Sutherland Norman

www.donnalnorman.com

Cover Artist: Kim C. Lee

www.kimclee.com

© 2023 DLN Leadership Group

Made in the USA
Columbia, SC
11 April 2023

853bf954-9f03-4f88-a82f-75fee77e4dffR01